Cruising the  INSIDE Passage

NCP
NATURAL COLOR PRODUCTIONS

NATURAL COLOR PRODUCTIONS
570 Ebury Place
New Westminster, B.C.
V3M 6M8
Telephone: (604) 521-1579
Printed by Lawson Mardon
International in Hong Kong.

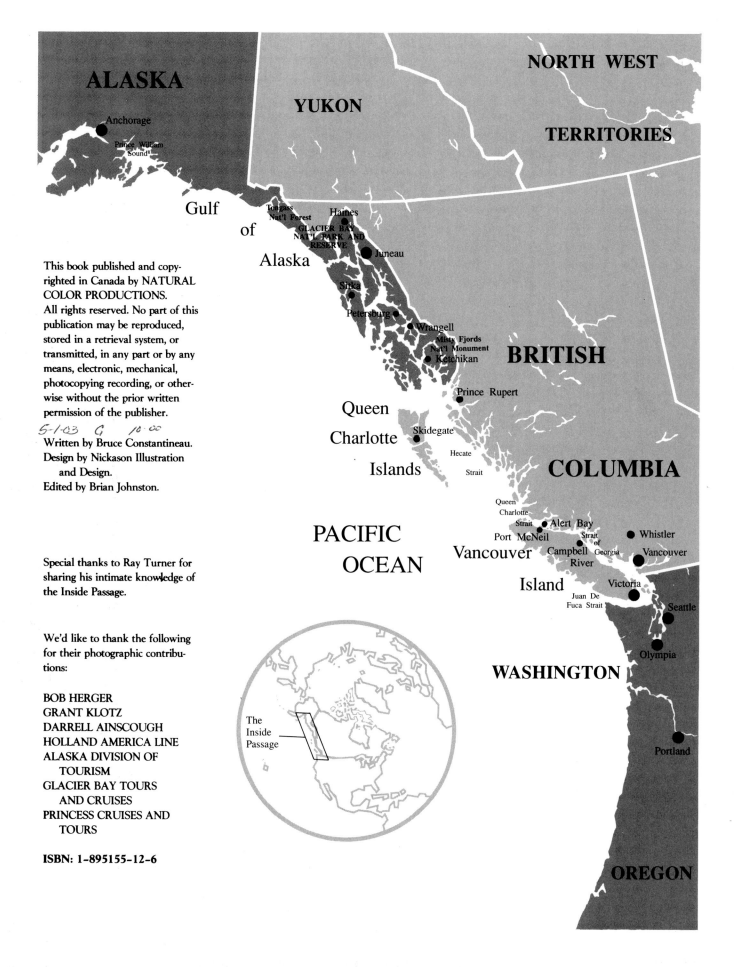

ALASKA

Anchorage

Prince William Sound

Gulf

of

Alaska

YUKON

NORTH WEST

TERRITORIES

Tongass Nat'l Forest

Haines

GLACIER BAY NAT'L PARK AND RESERVE

Juneau

Sitka

Petersburg

Wrangell

Misty Fjords Nat'l Monument

Ketchikan

Prince Rupert

BRITISH

Queen

Charlotte

Islands

Skidegate

Hecate

Strait

COLUMBIA

PACIFIC

OCEAN

Queen Charlotte Strait

Alert Bay

Port McNeil

Strait of Georgia

Whistler

Campbell River

Vancouver

Vancouver

Island

Victoria

Juan De Fuca Strait

WASHINGTON

Seattle

Olympia

Portland

OREGON

The Inside Passage

5-1-03   G   10.00

Written by Bruce Constantineau.
Design by Nickason Illustration and Design.
Edited by Brian Johnston.

Special thanks to Ray Turner for sharing his intimate knowledge of the Inside Passage.

We'd like to thank the following for their photographic contributions:

BOB HERGER
GRANT KLOTZ
DARRELL AINSCOUGH
HOLLAND AMERICA LINE
ALASKA DIVISION OF
    TOURISM
GLACIER BAY TOURS
    AND CRUISES
PRINCESS CRUISES AND
    TOURS

ISBN: 1–895155–12–6

Cruising the
INSIDE
Passage

A journey through the renowned Inside Passage of British Columbia and Alaska offers one of the most unique and awe-inspiring travel experiences on earth. Picture a thousand-mile, deep-channel waterway where eagles soar and migrating whales display their majestic beauty. Massive glaciers release huge chunks of ice that crash into the sea. Centuries-old native culture abounds in villages up and down the coastline. Combine all those elements with an unrivalled mountain-and-sea landscape and you can appreciate the sense of wonder that overwhelms visitors when they travel the same route taken by Capt. George Vancouver 200 years ago.

Above: Tlingit and Haida myths and legends displayed on totem poles at Totem Bight Totem Park in Ketchikan, Alaska.
Right: A cruise liner sails through waters bounded by spectacular mountain scenery.

In the late 1700s, four European nations actively explored the rugged coast of British Columbia and Alaska — Britain, Russia, France and Spain. Britain wanted a share of the lucrative fur trade and sought to find the "Northwest Passage," a fabled waterway thought to connect the Atlantic Ocean to the Pacific Ocean.

Russia wanted to expand its trade with China, where seal, fox and sea otter furs had become high fashion. France was also attracted by the trade possibilities while Spain wanted to

protect its longstanding interest in the region.

The most detailed charting of the Inside Passage was done by two British explorers — Capt. James Cook and Capt. George Vancouver.

Cook explored Prince William Sound and crossed through the Aleutian Island chain, reaching the Bering Strait between Alaska and Siberia. Vancouver sailed the Inside Passage waters to Queen Charlotte Sound and eventually reached the southern tip of the Alaska Panhandle.

Top Left: A native graveyard in Sitka. Religion was highly organized among Coastal Indians, with each having its own special spirits and dances.
Bottom Left: Historic Creek Street in Ketchikan, where houses are built on pilings overlooking Ketchikan Creek. The street was famous as a former red-light district.

Dolly's Historic Museum on Creek Street is the fully restored home of the area's most renowned resident — a lady named Dolly who was Ketchikan's last "madame."
Below: Visitor information centre in Anchorage.

Right: Horned puffins are expert swimmers and divers who feed mainly on fish. They nest in large colonies on rocky coasts during the breeding season in June and July.

Below: Mount Drum, more than 12,000 feet high, lies at the western edge of the Wrangell Mountains.

Opposite Page: A black bear holds a freshly caught pink salmon. Black bears can be seen along salmon streams, tidal grasslands or on high mountain meadows. They are skillful tree climbers and can run as fast as 25 mph when chasing prey.

Following Page: Glacial scenery in the Tatshenshini River.

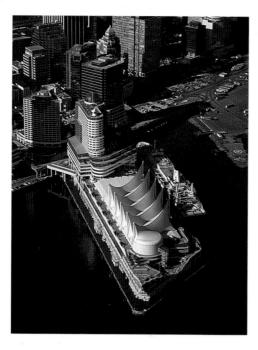

Canada Place, Vancouver's main cruise ship terminal, was built by the federal government at a cost of $145 million to serve as the Canadian Pavilion at Expo 86. It houses a world class trade and convention centre, the luxury Pan Pacific Hotel and a world trade centre. The building juts into Vancouver's harbour from the foot of Burrard Street and public promenade decks offer some of the finest harbour views in the city. Canada Place boasts five great white teflon sails which make the building appear ready to set sail for a voyage of its own.

Above: An aerial view of Canada Place, Vancouver's exciting connection to the downtown waterfront. Shops and restaurants are clustered at the northern end of the pier. *Right:* Canada Place lit up at night.

Vancouver, Canada's picturesque gateway to the Pacific, boasts a gorgeous setting and one of the busiest harbours in the world.

With a diverse population of more than 1.5 million people in the metropolitan area, Vancouver is renowned for its cosmopolitan shopping and dining experiences. The city's Chinatown district is the second largest in North America.

Vancouver is blessed with many parks and gardens and a stunning backdrop of Coast Range mountains.

Stanley Park, located at the western edge of the downtown core, contains 1,000 acres of cedar and fir forest, a zoo, an aquarium and a scenic seawall walk.

Vancouver started out as a hamlet called Gastown, named after a talkative saloon keeper known as "Gassy" Jack Deighton. Gastown was incorporated as the city of Vancouver in April 1886 but was destroyed by fire two months later. The residents quickly rebuilt their city and in 1887, it became the western terminal for the Canadian Pacific Railway.

Bottom Left: A cruise ship passes beneath Vancouver's Lions Gate Bridge. The famous suspension bridge, opened in 1938, provides a vital link between Vancouver and the North Shore communities.

Top left: A cruise liner heads out to sea after calling in Vancouver. The city's North Shore, The Lions Gate Bridge and the Coastal Range mountains provide a scenic backdrop.

Below: Downtown Vancouver and Burrard Inlet, the busiest port on the Pacific Coast of North America.

Victoria, which began as a Hudson's Bay Company fort in 1843, became the capital of British Columbia when the new province joined Canadian confederation in 1871.

With a distinctive English atmosphere, the city takes pride in its beautiful parks and flowers. Beacon Hill Park, a 154-acre site located near the downtown core, contains lakes, cricket grounds, a Royal Rose Garden and one of the world's tallest totem poles.

Visitors can tour the city on double-decker buses or on horse-drawn coaches. A tour woud include visits to the provincial Legislature and the famed Empress Hotel, both designed by master architect Francis Rattenbury. Other major attractions include Bastion Square, with its restored historic buildings, and the Royal British Columbia Museum.

Far Left: A native totem pole on display in Thunderbird Park near the Empress Hotel.

Bottom Left: Victoria's inner harbour serves as the focal point for most of the city's major landmarks.

Left: The world famous Butchart Gardens, located 12 miles north of Victoria in Brentwood. The five gardens on the Butchart family estate were created in 1904 after Mrs. Jennie Butchart decided to beautify the limestone quarry of her husband's cement factory.

Below: The Empress Hotel, built by the Canadian Pacific Railway, has been a city landmark since it opened in 1908. Afternoon tea at the Empress remains a must for many visitors.

Right: A totem pole on a sacred Kwakiutl burial ground near Alert Bay, at the northern end of Vancouver Island. The Kwakiutl and Nootka Indians got a relatively late start in carving totem poles, as none of the poles around Alert Bay was carved before 1890.

Below: A barren tree silhouetted against a dramatic sunset along the Inside Passage.

Opposite Page: A sandstone shoreline dominates a desolate beach on Calvert Island off the northern tip of Vancouver Island.

Following Page: The rocky shoreline around Whitecliff Island in Queen Charlotte Sound.

The Queen Charlotte Islands of British Columbia include about 150 islands south of the Alaska Panhandle that run in a north–south direction for about 160 miles. Capt. George Dixon explored the islands in 1787 and named them for his ship, the Queen Charlotte.

The rugged islands have mild winters because of warm ocean currents but the Queen Charlotte archipelago ranks among the wettest places on earth. The heavy annual rainfall produces huge rain forest that are deeply quilted with moss.

The Haida Indians, the original island settlers, are renowned for their craftsmanship, especially as canoe makers, house builders and wood carvers. Haida communities included highly organized social classes and a hereditary nobility.

Far Left: An overgrown Haida totem pole on the Queen Charlotte Islands.
Bottom Left: Skeletal remains on a sacred Haida burial ground. Cremation was relatively rare among the Haida, who sometimes deposited their dead in caves. They more frequently laid the dead in mortuary houses or placed the coffin on top of a carved post.
Left: A cluster of weathered Haida totem poles. Totem carvings depict the native ancestry, clan membership and history.
Below: Prince Rupert, located about 500 miles north of Vancouver, is Canada's northernmost ice-free port and the main trading centre for the northern B.C. coast.

lacier Bay National Park and Preserve features a spectacular 60-mile-long bay fed by a dozen mammoth glaciers at its upper end. When Russian explorers discovered the area in 1741, it was little more than a sheet of ice. By the time noted naturalist John Muir entered the bay in 1879, the ice front had retreated 48 miles and tidewaters invaded the basin, filling the deep, narrow fjords.

Glacier Bay offers visitors tremendous opportunities to witness one of the most dramatic sites of the Inside Passage — glacier "calving," where massive blocks of ice break loose from glaciers and crash into the sea.

Above: A colourful totem pole on display at Totem Bight Totem Park in Ketchikan.
Right: A cruise ship sails through a spectacular snow-capped mountain setting in Glacier Bay.

Right: Ketchikan's famed Creek Street, where homes built on pilings once served as the city's red-light district.
Below: A view of the cruise ship dock, Tongass Narrows and the city of Ketchikan from Cape Fox Hill.
Far Right: A Ketchikan view looking towards the mountain backdrop. Note the wooden stairs on the right.
Bottom Right: A cruise ship sailing Tongass Narrows.

Ketchikan, Alaska's fourth largest city, gives northbound sea travellers their first look at a major Alaskan community. Squeezed between the mountains and the sea, Ketchikan is long and narrow — several miles long but never more than 10 blocks wide.

The gold rush of 1898 turned Ketchikan into a busy mining town and it still retains a rustic feel, with wooden stairways and homes built on pilings. Ketchikan has the world's largest collection of totem poles, with several sites dedicated to this art form.

Right: A northern sea lion basks on a rocky point. Sea lions can grow to 11 feet in length and weigh up to 2,200 pounds.

Below: Misty Fjords National Monument. Once described as "the most spectacular and inspiring scenic portion of Alaska," the 9,300-square-kilometre area southeast of Ketchikan is one of the largest parklands in the United States.

Opposite Page: Sheer mountain cliffs jut from the water at Misty Fjords.

Following Page: An acrobatic gray whale heaves itself out of the water. Measuring up to 50 feet long, gray whales eat plankton, small fish and small animals.

Located near the mouth of the mighty Stikine River, Wrangell is Alaska's third oldest city and the only one to have flown three flags — Russian, British and American.

The Russians called it Fort St. Dionysius when it was first built in 1834. The British leased the area and renamed it Fort Stikine and the Americans called it Wrangell after the U.S. purchase of Alaska in 1867.

Three gold rushes in the 1800s brought settlers to the community and

it grew to become a major supply point for gold miners heading up the Stikine. Today, Wrangell is an important lumber exporting port and shrimp processing community and the area boasts excellent fishing.

Visitors to Wrangell can visit Chief Shakes Island to find an impressive collection of totem poles and a ceremonial house. Petroglyphs carved on rocks north of the ferry terminal are estimated to be more than 8,000 years old.

Left: Aerial view of Wrangell, Alaska. The city was named after Baron von Wrangell, a governor of the Russian-American Company, which built a fort on the site in 1834.
Bottom Left: A cruise liner sails through a typical Inside Passage setting.
Below: A commercial fishing seiner in Lynn Canal in southeast Alaska.

A highlight of any trip through the Inside Passage is the unique opportunity to experience the region's diverse native culture.

Northwest Coastal Indians were hunters and gatherers and highly dependent on the Pacific salmon as a food source. Natives clustered into villages near the mouths of salmon rivers or in bays frequented by seals, otters and other sea mammals.

The abundant food supply allowed them to establish permanent settlements and this permanency led to a culture as complex as any settled agricultural society.

Native society was divided according to hereditary rank and life was enriched by elaborate festivals and art.

The natives were divided into several language groups — Tlingit, Haida, Tsimshian, Kwakiutl, Bella Coola, Nootka and Coast Salish.

Far Left: A Tlingit totem carving in Sitka National Historical Park, a beautiful wooded area set aside for exhibits depicting native history and culture.

Bottom Left: The Cape Fox Dancers perform at the Beaver Tribal House in Saxman Totem Park. Visitors are encouraged to participate in the dance ceremony.

Left: A totem pole in Saxman Totem Park in Ketchikan. The park has 26 totem poles, a carving centre and a tribal house.

Below: Shakes Tribal House on Shakes Island, located in Wrangell's inner harbour. The island can be reached by a 15-minute walk from the ferry terminal.

Right: St. Nicholas Russian Orthodox Church, at the corner of Fifth and Gold Streets in Juneau, Alaska. Built in 1894, the frame building houses a dome, icons and various artifacts brought from Russia during the 19th century.

Below: The Alaska State Capitol building in Juneau is the hub of Alaska's government – housing both legislative branches, the Governor's office, the State Historical Library, the courts and other administrative agencies.

Far Right: The Governor's mansion in Juneau.

Bottom Right: Downtown Juneau, Alaska's capital city is surrounded by wilderness and is nestled between Gastineau Channel and Mounts Juneau and Roberts.

Right: A young bald eagle. The bird will not have its distinctive white head until it's about four years old.
Below: Mendenhall Glacier in Tongass National Forest near Juneau. The popular glacier is nearly three miles wide, 12 miles long and more than 200 feet high.
Following Page: Spectacular mountain scenery near Sitka.

Right: A Tlingit totem carving in Sitka National Historical Park.
Below: The Sitka Pioneers Home. Since 1934, it has served as a sanctuary for the hardy men and women who pioneered Alaska's frontier.
Far Right: Sitka area mountain scene.
Bottom Right: The Sitka waterfront. Sitka was the site of the first Russian settlement in southeast Alaska.

Sitka, first established by Russian Count Alexander Baranof in 1799, was wiped out by the Tlingit Indians in 1802 but reestablished by the Russians two years later.

Until the U.S. purchase of Alaska in 1867, Sitka served as the Czar's North American capital and it was known as New Archangel. For several years, Sitka was known as the "Paris of the Pacific."

St. Michael's Cathedral, with its impressive collection of Russian artifacts, is a popular Alaskan tourist attraction.

Above: Mount Edgecumbe near Sitka. The 10,500-foot peak is southeastern Alaska's only volcanic mountain. Located on Kruzof Island, the top of the mountain can be reached by trail.

Left: A sea lion dives into the water from its rocky perch.

*I*nside Passage waters host a variety of awe-inspiring whale species that can often be seen by visitors. Distinctive black and white killer whales — or Orcas — and long-flippered humpback whales are common summer visitors to the region. The minke, gray, finback, sei and blue whales also frequent the area. The blue whale is the world's largest mammal, weighing more than 100 tons and reaching lengths of 90 feet.

The ancestors of today's whales were land–dwelling, air–breathing mammals who successfully returned to the ocean to live. Many whale species are endangered and scientists now monitor their numbers closely.

Above: A humpback whale displays its enormous fluke — or tail fin — before disappearing beneath the ocean surface.
Right: The ice-filled waters of Glacier Bay reflect an impressive mountain backdrop.

Right: A Glacier Bay cruiser takes visitors to one of the most dramatic sights of any Inside Passage trip – glacial "calving," where massive slabs of ice break off from glaciers and crash into the sea in spectacular fashion. Some glaciers calve so much ice and create so much wave activity that it's rare to get within two miles of their ice cliffs.

Below: A tidewater glacier in Glacier Bay, where 12 glaciers actively calve icebergs into the bay.

Opposite Page: Water splashes at the base of a glacier giving up another iceberg.

Following Page: Johns Hopkins Inlet – Glacier Bay.

Alaska's stunning visual landscape was created by millions of years of glacial activity.

Glaciers, essentially slow moving rivers of ice, originate in the freezing tops of mountain ranges and flow down rocky valleys to lower regions. A glacier advances as long as it accumulates more snow and ice than it melts.

Advancing ice scrapes and grinds the boulders and gravel beneath it, pushing ahead huge ridges of rock and earth.

Some dramatic after–effects of glacial movement include sharp, pointed "horn" mountain peaks and fjords — long, narrow glacial troughs filled with sea water.

Throughout the world, glaciers and polar ice store more water than lakes, rivers, groundwater and the atmosphere combined.

Far Left: A curious sea otter pops its head above the water. Otters live close to shore and can be seen among kelp beds diving for sea urchins, abalone and mussels.
Bottom Left: McBride Glacier in the east arm of Muir Inlet near Glacier Bay.
Left: Mount Alyeska, a ski resort outside Anchorage.
Below: A lone seal basks on a rocky point in Glacier Bay National Park and Preserve. Seals feed on a variety of fish and crustaceans and groups of them can often be seen lying on sandbars or reefs.

Above: A cruise liner glides through the ice-filled waters of Glacier Bay.

Left: A harbour seal takes a break on a Glacier Bay ice flow. Harbour seals are the most common seal found in the Inside Passage waters.

*A*nchorage, Alaska's largest city and its main commercial and transportation centre, lies in the shadow of the Chugach Mountains on Cook Inlet.

Athabaskan, Haida and Tlingit Indians lived in the Anchorage area before white settlers arrived and founded the city in 1914 as the construction centre of the Alaska Railroad. It was originally known as Ship Creek and then Woodrow before it was renamed Anchorage in 1915.

Anchorage houses two major military installations and serves as the administrative centre of the state's lucrative oil industry.

Above: "The Last Blue Whale," an Anchorage art work produced by Joseph Princiotta.
Right: The Anchorage skyline, with the Chugach Mountains in the background. The city is a major Alaskan port.

Much of downtown Anchorage had to be rebuilt following a devastating 1964 earthquake that shook the city for five minutes. The quake killed 131 people and caused $750 million worth of damage, dropping parts of the downtown core 10 feet below the pre-quake street level.

Today, Anchorage is a modern, vibrant city where old mingles with new. Several historic buildings have been preserved and moved from their original locations to make way for skyscrapers.

City residents enjoy the best of both worlds — all the amenities of a big city plus unlimited recreational opportunities just minutes from home. Excellent skiing, hiking and fishing spots can be found close to the bustling city.

Anchorage enjoys a surprisingly mild climate, with winter temperatures normally ranging between 10 and 25 degrees Fahrenheit. The longest day of the year — in mid-June — offers Anchorage residents about 19 and a half hours of possible sunshine.

Left: Anchorage skyscrapers set against a dramatic orange sky. City nights can be as long as 18 and a half hours in the winter or as short as four and a half hours in the summer.
Bottom Left: Beautiful spring flowers in the Anchorage business district.
Below: Houses are dwarfed by Anchorage office towers near the downtown core.

Alaskan wildlife is as varied as the incredible landscape it inhabits. Great herds of caribou roam the treeless tundra of the Interior while huge Kodiak brown bears fish salmon streams in lush green forests.

Some of Alaska's major land mammal species include the bear, mountain goat, Dall sheep, bison, musk ox, black-tailed deer, reindeer and the largest member of the deer family — the moose. An adult bull moose can weigh up to 1,600 pounds and stand six feet high at the shoulder.

Wolves are common throughout the state and so are smaller animals like the otter, beaver, mink, weasel, fox, lynx and rabbit.

Alaska is also a refuge for nearly 400 species of birds and more bald eagles live in the state than in all other U.S. states combined.

Far Left: A moose grazes in a mountain meadow in Denali National Park and Preserve. Moose are abundant throughout the Cook Inlet area, from the Kenai Peninsula to the Alaska Range.
Bottom Left: Snowy mountains in the Denali region of Alaska's Interior.
Left: Grassy marshlands contrast with mountainous terrain near Valdez.
Below: Tidewater glaciers join forces with snow-dusted mountains to create an inspiring setting near Valdez. The Valdez region, nestled between majestic alpine mountains and scenic Prince William Sound, has been called "the Switzerland of Alaska."

Right: Rugged, horn-peaked mountains jut skyward in Denali National Park.
Bottom Right: Denali mountains with Mt. McKinley in background.
Far Right: A bull moose searches for food in Denali National Park.
Below: Still, quiet waters in the Denali region.
Following Page: Columbia Glacier in Prince William Sound.

More than half of all protected parklands in the United States are currently found in Alaska, as preservation of the state's unique environment remains a major goal of the state and federal governments.

One of the most popular parks in Alaska is Denali National Park and Preserve, which surrounds North America's highest mountain — Mt. McKinley. Denali is the Indian name for the peak, meaning "The Great One."

As well, seventeen of the 20 highest mountains in the United States are found in Alaska.